Are you enjoying this awesome Podcast Planner?

If so, please leave us a review. We are very interested in your feedback to create even better products for you to enjoy soon.

Shopping for Podcast Planners can be fun.
Visit our website at amazing-notebooks.com or scan the QR code below to see all of our awesome and creative products!

Thank you very much!

Amazing Podcast Planners
www.amazing-notebooks.com
Copyright © 2020. All rights reserved.

No part of this book or this book as a whole may be used, reproduced, or transmitted in any form or means without written permission from the publisher

Welcome to Your Podcast Planner

Name ....

Phone ....

Email ....

Brain Dump

Brain Dump

Brain Dump

Podcast Name _____ **Episode #** _____

Recording Date _____ **Broadcast Date** _____

Recording Location _____

Host(s) _____

Guest(s) _____ **Fee?** _____

Main Feature _____

Running Order

Time Stamp	Segment

Music / FX _____

Contest

Sponsor _____

Prize _____

Winner _____

Talking Points

_____

_____

_____

Topic to discuss:

Hosts:

Description:

To Do List:
- [ ]
- [ ]
- [ ]
- [ ]
- [ ]
- [ ]

Notes:

My Ideal Listener:

Segments

Comments & Notes

Conclusion / Review

I Need to Practice:

I Didn`t Expect:

I Enjoyed:

Podcast Name _____ **Episode #** _____

Recording Date _____ **Broadcast Date** _____

Recording Location _____

Host(s) _____

Guest(s) _____ **Fee?** _____

Main Feature _____

Running Order

Time Stamp	Segment

Music / FX _____

Contest

Sponsor _____

Prize _____

Winner _____

Talking Points

_____

_____

_____

Topic to discuss:

Hosts:

Description:

To Do List:
- ☐
- ☐
- ☐
- ☐
- ☐
- ☐

Notes:

My Ideal Listener:

Segments

Comments & Notes

Conclusion / Review

I Need to Practice:

I Didn`t Expect:

I Enjoyed:

Podcast Name _____ **Episode #** _____

Recording Date _____ **Broadcast Date** _____

Recording Location _____

Host(s) _____

Guest(s) _____ **Fee?** _____

Main Feature _____

Running Order

Time Stamp	Segment

Music / FX _____

Contest

Sponsor _____

Prize _____

Winner _____

Talking Points

_____

_____

_____

Topic to discuss:

Hosts:

Description:

To Do List:
- [ ]
- [ ]
- [ ]
- [ ]
- [ ]
- [ ]

Notes:

My Ideal Listener:

Segments

Comments & Notes

Conclusion / Review

I Need to Practice:

I Didn`t Expect:

I Enjoyed:

Podcast Name _____   **Episode #** _____

Recording Date _____   **Broadcast Date** _____

Recording Location _____

Host(s) _____

Guest(s) _____   **Fee?** _____

Main Feature _____

Running Order

Time Stamp	Segment

Music / FX _____

Contest

Sponsor _____

Prize _____

Winner _____

Talking Points

_____

_____

_____

Topic to discuss:

_____
_____
_____

Hosts:

_____

Description: **To Do List:**

_____   ☐ _____
_____   ☐ _____
_____   ☐ _____
_____   ☐ _____
_____   ☐ _____
_____   ☐ _____

Notes:

_____
_____
_____
_____
_____
_____

My Ideal Listener:

_____
_____
_____
_____
_____
_____

Segments

Comments & Notes

Conclusion / Review

I Need to Practice:

I Didn't Expect:

I Enjoyed:

Podcast Name _____   **Episode #** _____

Recording Date _____   **Broadcast Date** _____

Recording Location _____

Host(s) _____

Guest(s) _____   **Fee?** _____

Main Feature _____

Running Order

Time Stamp	Segment

Music / FX _____

Contest

Sponsor _____

Prize _____

Winner _____

Talking Points

_____

_____

_____

Topic to discuss:

Hosts:

Description:

To Do List:
- [ ]
- [ ]
- [ ]
- [ ]
- [ ]
- [ ]

Notes:

My Ideal Listener:

Segments

Comments & Notes

Conclusion / Review

I Need to Practice:

I Didn`t Expect:

I Enjoyed:

Podcast Name _____ **Episode #** _____

Recording Date _____ **Broadcast Date** _____

Recording Location _____

Host(s) _____

Guest(s) _____ **Fee?** _____

Main Feature _____

Running Order

Time Stamp	Segment

Music / FX _____

Contest

Sponsor _____

Prize _____

Winner _____

Talking Points

_____
_____
_____
_____

Topic to discuss:

Hosts:

Description:

To Do List:
- [ ]
- [ ]
- [ ]
- [ ]
- [ ]
- [ ]

Notes:

My Ideal Listener:

Segments

Comments & Notes

Conclusion / Review

I Need to Practice:

I Didn't Expect:

I Enjoyed:

Podcast Name _____   **Episode #** _____

Recording Date _____   **Broadcast Date** _____

Recording Location _____

Host(s) _____

Guest(s) _____   **Fee?** _____

Main Feature _____

Running Order

Time Stamp	Segment

Music / FX _____

Contest

Sponsor _____

Prize _____

Winner _____

Talking Points

_____

_____

_____

_____

Topic to discuss:

Hosts:

Description:

To Do List:
- [ ]
- [ ]
- [ ]
- [ ]
- [ ]
- [ ]

Notes:

My Ideal Listener:

Segments

Comments & Notes

Conclusion / Review

I Need to Practice:

I Didn`t Expect:

I Enjoyed:

Podcast Name _____ **Episode #** _____

Recording Date _____ **Broadcast Date** _____

Recording Location _____

Host(s) _____

Guest(s) _____ **Fee?** _____

Main Feature _____

Running Order

Time Stamp	Segment

Music / FX _____

Contest

Sponsor _____

Prize _____

Winner _____

Talking Points

_____

_____

_____

Topic to discuss:

Hosts:

Description:

To Do List:
- [ ]
- [ ]
- [ ]
- [ ]
- [ ]
- [ ]

Notes:

My Ideal Listener:

Segments

Comments & Notes

Conclusion / Review

I Need to Practice:

I Didn`t Expect:

I Enjoyed:

Podcast Name _____ **Episode #** _____

Recording Date _____ **Broadcast Date** _____

Recording Location _____

Host(s) _____

Guest(s) _____ **Fee?** _____

Main Feature _____

Running Order

Time Stamp	Segment

Music / FX _____

Contest

Sponsor _____

Prize _____

Winner _____

Talking Points

_____

_____

_____

Topic to discuss:

Hosts:

Description:

To Do List:
- ☐
- ☐
- ☐
- ☐
- ☐
- ☐

Notes:

My Ideal Listener:

Segments

Comments & Notes

Conclusion / Review

I Need to Practice:

I Didn`t Expect:

I Enjoyed:

Podcast Name _____ **Episode #** _____

Recording Date _____ **Broadcast Date** _____

Recording Location _____

Host(s) _____

Guest(s) _____ **Fee?** _____

Main Feature _____

Running Order

Time Stamp	Segment

Music / FX _____

Contest

Sponsor _____

Prize _____

Winner _____

Talking Points

_____

_____

_____

Topic to discuss:

Hosts:

Description:

To Do List:
- [ ]
- [ ]
- [ ]
- [ ]
- [ ]
- [ ]

Notes:

My Ideal Listener:

Segments

Comments & Notes

Conclusion / Review

I Need to Practice:

I Didn`t Expect:

I Enjoyed:

Podcast Name _____   **Episode #** _____

Recording Date _____   **Broadcast Date** _____

Recording Location _____

Host(s) _____

Guest(s) _____   **Fee?** _____

Main Feature _____

Running Order

Time Stamp	Segment

Music / FX _____

Contest

Sponsor _____

Prize _____

Winner _____

Talking Points

_____

_____

_____

Topic to discuss:

Hosts:

Description:

To Do List:
- [ ]
- [ ]
- [ ]
- [ ]
- [ ]
- [ ]

Notes:

My Ideal Listener:

Segments

Comments & Notes

Conclusion / Review

I Need to Practice:

I Didn't Expect:

I Enjoyed:

Brain Dump

Brain Dump

Brain Dump

Podcast Name _____ **Episode #** _____

Recording Date _____ **Broadcast Date** _____

Recording Location _____

Host(s) _____

Guest(s) _____ **Fee?** _____

Main Feature _____

Running Order

Time Stamp	Segment

Music / FX _____

Contest

Sponsor _____

Prize _____

Winner _____

Talking Points

_____

_____

_____

Topic to discuss:

Hosts:

Description:

To Do List:
- [ ]
- [ ]
- [ ]
- [ ]
- [ ]
- [ ]

Notes:

My Ideal Listener:

Segments

Comments & Notes

Conclusion / Review

I Need to Practice:

I Didn`t Expect:

I Enjoyed:

Podcast Name _____ **Episode #** _____

Recording Date _____ **Broadcast Date** _____

Recording Location _____

Host(s) _____

Guest(s) _____ **Fee?** _____

Main Feature _____

Running Order

Time Stamp	Segment

Music / FX _____

Contest

Sponsor _____

Prize _____

Winner _____

Talking Points

_____
_____
_____
_____

Topic to discuss:

_____
_____
_____
_____

Hosts:

_____

Description:

_____
_____
_____
_____

To Do List:

- [ ] _____
- [ ] _____
- [ ] _____
- [ ] _____
- [ ] _____
- [ ] _____

Notes:

_____
_____
_____
_____
_____

My Ideal Listener:

_____
_____
_____
_____
_____
_____

Segments

Comments & Notes

Conclusion / Review

I Need to Practice:

I Didn't Expect:

I Enjoyed:

Podcast Name _____ **Episode #** _____

Recording Date _____ **Broadcast Date** _____

Recording Location _____

Host(s) _____

Guest(s) _____ **Fee?** _____

Main Feature _____

Running Order

Time Stamp	Segment

Music / FX _____

Contest

Sponsor _____

Prize _____

Winner _____

Talking Points

Topic to discuss:

Hosts:

Description:

To Do List:
- ☐
- ☐
- ☐
- ☐
- ☐
- ☐

Notes:

My Ideal Listener:

Segments

Comments & Notes

Conclusion / Review

I Need to Practice:

I Didn`t Expect:

I Enjoyed:

Podcast Name _____ **Episode #** _____

Recording Date _____ **Broadcast Date** _____

Recording Location _____

Host(s) _____

Guest(s) _____ **Fee?** _____

Main Feature _____

Running Order

Time Stamp	Segment

Music / FX _____

Contest

Sponsor _____

Prize _____

Winner _____

Talking Points

_____

_____

_____

Topic to discuss:

Hosts:

Description:

To Do List:
- [ ]
- [ ]
- [ ]
- [ ]
- [ ]
- [ ]

Notes:

My Ideal Listener:

Segments

Comments & Notes

Conclusion / Review

I Need to Practice:

I Didn't Expect:

I Enjoyed:

Podcast Name _____ **Episode #** _____

Recording Date _____ **Broadcast Date** _____

Recording Location _____

Host(s) _____

Guest(s) _____ **Fee?** _____

Main Feature _____

Running Order

Time Stamp	Segment

Music / FX _____

Contest

Sponsor _____

Prize _____

Winner _____

Talking Points

_____

_____

_____

_____

Topic to discuss:

Hosts:

Description:

To Do List:
- [ ]
- [ ]
- [ ]
- [ ]
- [ ]
- [ ]

Notes:

My Ideal Listener:

Segments

Comments & Notes

Conclusion / Review

I Need to Practice:

I Didn`t Expect:

I Enjoyed:

Podcast Name _____ **Episode #** _____

Recording Date _____ **Broadcast Date** _____

Recording Location _____

Host(s) _____

Guest(s) _____ **Fee?** _____

Main Feature _____

Running Order

Time Stamp	Segment

Music / FX _____

Contest

Sponsor _____

Prize _____

Winner _____

Talking Points

_____

_____

_____

Topic to discuss:

_____
_____
_____
_____

Hosts:

_____

Description:

_____
_____
_____
_____
_____

To Do List:

☐
☐
☐
☐
☐
☐

Notes:

_____
_____
_____
_____
_____
_____

My Ideal Listener:

_____
_____
_____
_____
_____
_____

Segments

Comments & Notes

Conclusion / Review

I Need to Practice:

I Didn`t Expect:

I Enjoyed:

Podcast Name _____ **Episode #** _____

Recording Date _____ **Broadcast Date** _____

Recording Location _____

Host(s) _____

Guest(s) _____ **Fee?** _____

Main Feature _____

Running Order

Time Stamp	Segment

Music / FX _____

Contest

Sponsor _____

Prize _____

Winner _____

Talking Points

_____

_____

_____

Topic to discuss:

Hosts:

Description:

To Do List:
- [ ]
- [ ]
- [ ]
- [ ]
- [ ]
- [ ]

Notes:

My Ideal Listener:

Segments

Comments & Notes

Conclusion / Review

I Need to Practice:

I Didn`t Expect:

I Enjoyed:

Podcast Name _____ **Episode #** _____

Recording Date _____ **Broadcast Date** _____

Recording Location _____

Host(s) _____

Guest(s) _____ **Fee?** _____

Main Feature _____

Running Order

Time Stamp	Segment

Music / FX _____

Contest

Sponsor _____

Prize _____

Winner _____

Talking Points

_____

_____

_____

Topic to discuss:

Hosts:

Description:

To Do List:
- [ ]
- [ ]
- [ ]
- [ ]
- [ ]
- [ ]

Notes:

My Ideal Listener:

Segments

Comments & Notes

Conclusion / Review

I Need to Practice:

I Didn't Expect:

I Enjoyed:

Podcast Name _____ **Episode #** _____

Recording Date _____ **Broadcast Date** _____

Recording Location _____

Host(s) _____

Guest(s) _____ **Fee?** _____

Main Feature _____

Running Order

Time Stamp	Segment

Music / FX _____

Contest

Sponsor _____

Prize _____

Winner _____

Talking Points

_____

_____

_____

Topic to discuss:

Hosts:

Description:

To Do List:
- [ ]
- [ ]
- [ ]
- [ ]
- [ ]
- [ ]

Notes:

My Ideal Listener:

Segments

Comments & Notes

Conclusion / Review

I Need to Practice:

I Didn't Expect:

I Enjoyed:

Podcast Name _____ **Episode #** _____

Recording Date _____ **Broadcast Date** _____

Recording Location _____

Host(s) _____

Guest(s) _____ **Fee?** _____

Main Feature _____

Running Order

Time Stamp	Segment

Music / FX _____

Contest

Sponsor _____

Prize _____

Winner _____

Talking Points

Topic to discuss:

Hosts:

Description:

To Do List:
- [ ]
- [ ]
- [ ]
- [ ]
- [ ]
- [ ]

Notes:

My Ideal Listener:

Segments

Comments & Notes

Conclusion / Review

I Need to Practice:

I Didn`t Expect:

I Enjoyed:

Podcast Name _____   **Episode #** _____

Recording Date _____   Broadcast Date _____

Recording Location _____

Host(s) _____

Guest(s) _____   Fee? _____

Main Feature _____

Running Order

Time Stamp	Segment

Music / FX _____

Contest

Sponsor _____

Prize _____

Winner _____

Talking Points

_____

_____

_____

Topic to discuss:

Hosts:

Description:

To Do List:
- [ ]
- [ ]
- [ ]
- [ ]
- [ ]
- [ ]

Notes:

My Ideal Listener:

Segments

Comments & Notes

Conclusion / Review

I Need to Practice:

I Didn`t Expect:

I Enjoyed:

Brain Dump

Brain Dump

Brain Dump

Podcast Name _____ **Episode #** _____

Recording Date _____ **Broadcast Date** _____

Recording Location _____

Host(s) _____

Guest(s) _____ **Fee?** _____

Main Feature _____

Running Order

Time Stamp	Segment

Music / FX _____

Contest

Sponsor _____

Prize _____

Winner _____

Talking Points

_____
_____
_____
_____

Topic to discuss:

Hosts:

Description:

To Do List:
- [ ]
- [ ]
- [ ]
- [ ]
- [ ]
- [ ]

Notes:

My Ideal Listener:

Segments

Comments & Notes

Conclusion / Review

I Need to Practice:

I Didn`t Expect:

I Enjoyed:

Podcast Name _____   **Episode #** _____

Recording Date _____   **Broadcast Date** _____

Recording Location _____

Host(s) _____

Guest(s) _____   **Fee?** _____

Main Feature _____

Running Order

Time Stamp	Segment

Music / FX _____

Contest

Sponsor _____

Prize _____

Winner _____

Talking Points

_____

_____

_____

Topic to discuss:

_____
_____
_____
_____

Hosts:

_____

Description:

_____
_____
_____
_____
_____

To Do List:

☐ _____
☐ _____
☐ _____
☐ _____
☐ _____
☐ _____

Notes:

_____
_____
_____
_____
_____
_____

My Ideal Listener:

_____
_____
_____
_____
_____
_____

Segments

Comments & Notes

Conclusion / Review

I Need to Practice:

I Didn`t Expect:

I Enjoyed:

Podcast Name _____   **Episode #** _____

Recording Date _____   **Broadcast Date** _____

Recording Location _____

Host(s) _____

Guest(s) _____   **Fee?** _____

Main Feature _____

Running Order

Time Stamp	Segment

Music / FX _____

Contest

Sponsor _____

Prize _____

Winner _____

Talking Points

_____

_____

_____

_____

Topic to discuss:

Hosts:

Description:

To Do List:
- ☐
- ☐
- ☐
- ☐
- ☐
- ☐

Notes:

My Ideal Listener:

Segments

Comments & Notes

Conclusion / Review

I Need to Practice:

I Didn't Expect:

I Enjoyed:

Podcast Name _____ **Episode #** _____

Recording Date _____ **Broadcast Date** _____

Recording Location _____

Host(s) _____

Guest(s) _____ **Fee?** _____

Main Feature _____

Running Order

Time Stamp	Segment

Music / FX _____

Contest

Sponsor _____

Prize _____

Winner _____

Talking Points

_____

_____

_____

Topic to discuss:

Hosts:

Description:

To Do List:
- [ ]
- [ ]
- [ ]
- [ ]
- [ ]
- [ ]

Notes:

My Ideal Listener:

Segments

_____
_____
_____
_____
_____

Comments & Notes

_____
_____
_____
_____
_____
_____

Conclusion / Review

I Need to Practice:

_____
_____
_____
_____

I Didn`t Expect:

_____
_____
_____

I Enjoyed:

_____
_____
_____

Podcast Name _____ **Episode #** _____

Recording Date _____ **Broadcast Date** _____

Recording Location _____

Host(s) _____

Guest(s) _____ **Fee?** _____

Main Feature _____

Running Order

Time Stamp	Segment

Music / FX _____

Contest

Sponsor _____

Prize _____

Winner _____

Talking Points

_____

_____

_____

Topic to discuss:

_____
_____
_____
_____

Hosts:
_____

Description:

_____
_____
_____
_____
_____

To Do List:
- [ ] _____
- [ ] _____
- [ ] _____
- [ ] _____
- [ ] _____
- [ ] _____

Notes:

_____
_____
_____
_____
_____
_____
_____

My Ideal Listener:

_____
_____
_____
_____
_____
_____
_____

Segments

Comments & Notes

Conclusion / Review

I Need to Practice:

I Didn't Expect:

I Enjoyed:

Podcast Name _____ **Episode #** _____

Recording Date _____ **Broadcast Date** _____

Recording Location _____

Host(s) _____

Guest(s) _____ Fee? _____

Main Feature _____

Running Order

Time Stamp	Segment

Music / FX _____

Contest

Sponsor _____

Prize _____

Winner _____

Talking Points

_____

_____

_____

Topic to discuss:

Hosts:

Description:

To Do List:
- [ ]
- [ ]
- [ ]
- [ ]
- [ ]
- [ ]

Notes:

My Ideal Listener:

Segments

Comments & Notes

Conclusion / Review

I Need to Practice:

I Didn`t Expect:

I Enjoyed:

Podcast Name _____ **Episode #** _____

Recording Date _____ **Broadcast Date** _____

Recording Location _____

Host(s) _____

Guest(s) _____ **Fee?** _____

Main Feature _____

Running Order

Time Stamp	Segment

Music / FX _____

Contest

Sponsor _____

Prize _____

Winner _____

Talking Points

_____

_____

_____

_____

Topic to discuss:

Hosts:

Description:

To Do List:
- [ ]
- [ ]
- [ ]
- [ ]
- [ ]
- [ ]

Notes:

My Ideal Listener:

Segments

Comments & Notes

Conclusion / Review

I Need to Practice:

I Didn`t Expect:

I Enjoyed:

Podcast Name _____ **Episode #** _____

Recording Date _____ **Broadcast Date** _____

Recording Location _____

Host(s) _____

Guest(s) _____ **Fee?** _____

Main Feature _____

Running Order

Time Stamp	Segment

Music / FX _____

Contest

Sponsor _____

Prize _____

Winner _____

Talking Points

_____

_____

_____

_____

Topic to discuss:

Hosts:

Description:

To Do List:
- [ ]
- [ ]
- [ ]
- [ ]
- [ ]
- [ ]

Notes:

My Ideal Listener:

Segments

Comments & Notes

Conclusion / Review

I Need to Practice:

I Didn`t Expect:

I Enjoyed:

Podcast Name _____ **Episode #** _____

Recording Date _____ **Broadcast Date** _____

Recording Location _____

Host(s) _____

Guest(s) _____ **Fee?** _____

Main Feature _____

Running Order

Time Stamp	Segment

Music / FX _____

Contest

Sponsor _____

Prize _____

Winner _____

Talking Points

_____

_____

_____

Topic to discuss:

Hosts:

Description:

To Do List:
- [ ]
- [ ]
- [ ]
- [ ]
- [ ]
- [ ]

Notes:

My Ideal Listener:

Segments

Comments & Notes

Conclusion / Review

I Need to Practice:

I Didn't Expect:

I Enjoyed:

Podcast Name _____ **Episode #** _____

Recording Date _____ **Broadcast Date** _____

Recording Location _____

Host(s) _____

Guest(s) _____ **Fee?** _____

Main Feature _____

Running Order

Time Stamp	Segment

Music / FX _____

Contest

Sponsor _____

Prize _____

Winner _____

Talking Points

Topic to discuss:

_____
_____
_____
_____

Hosts:

_____

Description:

_____
_____
_____
_____
_____

To Do List:

☐
☐
☐
☐
☐
☐

Notes:

_____
_____
_____
_____
_____
_____

My Ideal Listener:

_____
_____
_____
_____
_____
_____

Segments

Comments & Notes

Conclusion / Review

I Need to Practice:

I Didn`t Expect:

I Enjoyed:

Podcast Name _____   **Episode #** _____

Recording Date _____   **Broadcast Date** _____

Recording Location _____

Host(s) _____

Guest(s) _____   **Fee?** _____

Main Feature _____

Running Order

Time Stamp	Segment

Music / FX _____

Contest

Sponsor _____

Prize _____

Winner _____

Talking Points

_____

_____

_____

Topic to discuss:

Hosts:

Description:

To Do List:
- [ ]
- [ ]
- [ ]
- [ ]
- [ ]
- [ ]

Notes:

My Ideal Listener:

Segments

Comments & Notes

Conclusion / Review

I Need to Practice:

I Didn't Expect:

I Enjoyed:

Podcast Name _____ **Episode #** _____

Recording Date _____ **Broadcast Date** _____

Recording Location _____

Host(s) _____

Guest(s) _____ **Fee?** _____

Main Feature _____

Running Order

Time Stamp	Segment

Music / FX _____

Contest

Sponsor _____

Prize _____

Winner _____

Talking Points

_____
_____
_____
_____

Topic to discuss:

Hosts:

Description:

To Do List:
- [ ]
- [ ]
- [ ]
- [ ]
- [ ]
- [ ]

Notes:

My Ideal Listener:

Segments

Comments & Notes

Conclusion / Review

I Need to Practice:

I Didn`t Expect:

I Enjoyed:

Are you enjoying this awesome Podcast Planner?

If so, please leave us a review. We are very interested in your feedback to create even better products for you to enjoy soon.

Shopping for Podcast Planners can be fun.
Visit our website at amazing-notebooks.com or scan the QR code below to see all of our awesome and creative products!

Thank you very much!

Amazing Podcast Planners
www.amazing-notebooks.com
Copyright © 2020. All rights reserved.

No part of this book or this book as a whole may be used, reproduced, or transmitted in any form or means without written permission from the publisher

Made in the USA
Monee, IL
19 December 2023

50059616R00066